DRAW PEOPLE

IN 15 MINUTES

AMAZE YOUR FRIENDS WITH YOUR DRAWING SKILLS

DRAW PEOPLE

IN 15 MINUTES

JAKE SPICER

ilex

DRAW PEOPLE IN 15 MINUTES

An Hachette UK Company
www.hachette.co.uk

First published in the United Kingdom in 2014 by
ILEX, a division of Octopus Publishing Group Ltd
Octopus Publishing Group
Carmelite House
50 Victoria Embankment
London, EC4Y 0DZ
www.octopusbooks.co.uk

Design, layout, and text copyright
© Octopus Publishing Group 2014

Publisher: Alastair Campbell
Executive Publisher: Roly Allen
Editorial Director: Nick Jones
Senior Project Editor: Natalia Price-Cabrera
Senior Specialist Editor: Frank Gallaugher
Assistant Editor: Rachel Silverlight
Commissioning Editor: Zara Larcombe
Art Director: Julie Weir
Designers: Grade Design
Senior Production Manager: Katherine Hockley

ISBN: 978-1-78157-208-5

A CIP catalogue record for this book is available from the British Library

Printed and bound in China

10 9 8 7 6 5 4 3 2

Contents

Introduction

Drawing is for everybody. Anyone can learn to draw, and anybody who can draw can always learn to draw better. In a world of secondary images the process of drawing gives us precious moments to look at another person and create a response to them with marks on a tactile surface. Although some people have a natural aptitude for drawing, the ability to draw isn't a talent that you are born with; it's a skill that can be learned like playing a musical instrument or learning another language.

Drawing People

We draw subjects that engage us, and we find other people fascinating. The urge to draw ourselves and one another predates writing: from the walls of caves and the pyramids, to the sketchbooks of great thinkers and the canvases of great painters, the human figure is the most enduring artistic subject. This book is a practical guide to drawing people, focusing on the fundamental skills needed to make a quick sketch from life or a longer study from a reference or model. The aim isn't to give you templates for different figures and poses, but to provide the instruction you need to start really looking at other people and to simplify the complexity of the human form into clear, concise marks. Learning to draw is a skill for life and once you can draw the human figure any other subject is comparatively simple!

Why Draw?

You might draw as a hobby, to please yourself, or as a way to impress friends with a neat skill; you might draw to communicate ideas at work in anything from carpentry to web design. Whatever your reason for drawing you'll find that the more you draw and the better you get, the more you realize it's not just about making a picture on a piece of paper, but learning to see the world in a different way. The draftsman's eye sees wonder in the mundane; to be able to see something and translate that observation into a drawing is a skill with more facets to it than simply art or illusion.

The Language of Drawing

Drawing is a kind of visual language; a way of describing the observed world using a vocabulary of line and tone. Like a spoken language it has a certain grammar and structure that can be learned, developed, and adapted to suit the figures you want to sketch. This book serves as a guidebook, giving you some simple visual phrases for communicating fundamental elements of a figure; through practice and regular drawing you can develop a broader range and personal style. In time your marks can become poetic, eloquent, and you will become more fluid in your articulation, your visual description of what you see.

Beginning

As kids we all draw and paint, but as teenagers we can become so self-conscious about drawing that by adulthood we have talked ourselves out of it altogether. We can all reclaim the skill of drawing. When you first learn to draw you may feel clumsy, your pencil stumbling over lines as your tongue might stumble through a foreign phrase. There aren't some people who find drawing effortless and others who find it difficult: everybody struggles at first. The frustration that can accompany drawing is part of the discovery process; it encourages you to seek, be curious and to look harder at your subject. Without a certain amount of struggle no learning would take place, so be gentle with yourself and stick with it.

Before launching into the drawing chapters it's worth reading the next few pages. They serve as an introduction to drawing and a key to using the book. Enjoy.

Draw People in 15 Minutes

The 15-Minute Figure
The aim of this book is to give you practical advice that can be adapted to suit your needs. There are no right or wrong ways to draw, but there are better and worse ways of achieving certain kinds of drawings. To make a confident representational sketch of another person you need sound observational skills and clear, concise mark-making. What you do with those skills once you've learned them is limitless!

Why 15 Minutes?
It takes time to learn to draw well, but it needn't take long to pick up the basic skills. Good drawings aren't always the ones that you've spent a lot of time over; some of the best drawings are swift, energetic studies that capture the feel of the subject in a few well-placed lines. This book focuses on the core skills of drawing people, all of which can be brought into play in a fifteen-minute study. A quarter of an hour is all you need to make a competent, engaging sketch of a simple figure and practicing studies of that length will build the skills you need to make swifter, shorter studies or longer, more developed drawings. That said, we all work at a different pace; the important thing isn't how long you take to finish a drawing, but how much you learn from the process of making it.

Make Time to Learn
If you're learning from scratch you'll have sharpened plenty of pencils to stumps before you really start to be happy with your drawings; learning to draw takes curiosity and application. It's a personal and open-ended journey limited only by the time you can put in and your enthusiasm for your subject matter. If you spend even five minutes drawing every day you'll make noticeable progress in a few weeks. Find time to draw for three hours each week and after a year you'll be able to do things you hadn't thought possible before: a year is not a long time! You never stop learning, so you should enjoy the process and accept that your drawings won't always turn out as you'll hope. You need to make a lot of bad drawings before you make one good one.

How to Use the Book

This book is intended as a companion along the road of learning. It is not intended to teach you to draw, so much as to help you teach yourself to draw. Here is a key to the following chapters.

CHAPTER 2: WHAT YOU NEED

This chapter deals with drawing materials and with the practicalities of drawing from models, real life and from photographs. If you already feel confident with the materials you use and know who your subject will be, feel free to skip ahead.

CHAPTERS 3: ABOUT DRAWING

This chapter explains the drawing theory that underpins this book: it will be useful to return to this once you have done more practical drawing. Read Attitudes and Techniques to gain an initial insight into the drawing process.

CHAPTER 4: BUILDING SKILLS

Just like musicians practicing scales, even the experienced draftsman needs to work on their basic skills. This section is full of exercises to get you started in drawing, and to practice core skills once you are more experienced. At the end of the chapter the techniques in the main tutorial are explained.

CHAPTER 5: THE 15-MINUTE FIGURE

Speaks for itself: a step-by-step tutorial guiding you through drawing a clothed figure.

CHAPTER 6: GOING INTO DETAIL

This chapter is full of spotlights on tricky areas of the human figure. Dip in and out of it to help solve problems in your drawings.

WHAT YOU NEED

Your Materials

Drawing is a tactile process and the materials used to make a drawing are key to its success. A well-executed drawing made with poor implements on the wrong paper just isn't a good drawing. The techniques described in this book can broadly be applied to all drawing materials; you'll find you'll need to adapt the approaches for different media.

Always start simple; pencil and charcoal are staples of drawing because they are so versatile. Over time you'll find the best materials; experiment with different drawing materials and papers before you settle on a combination you like. Once you find something you get on well with, be fussy and don't settle for less than the ideal but equally don't be afraid to continue innovating and experimenting. The following pages contain more details on basic materials.

Pick Your Kit

If you want to get started straight away, here's a good basic kit list to begin with. It's what I've used for the drawings in this book:

HB, 2B, and 5B graphite pencils for a broad tonal range
A good quality pencil sharpener
A plastic eraser cut in half to give a sharp edge
Off-white size B drawing paper fixed to a drawing board
(95lb. or 140 gsm), or a sketchbook of the same paper

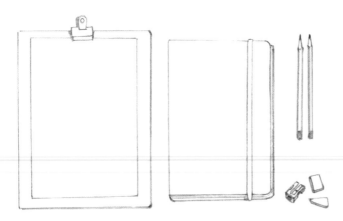

Paper

You need a paper that suits your drawing materials; the tone, color and surface texture will make a real difference to how your marks appear.

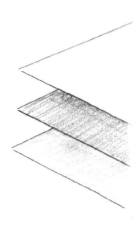

TYPE OF PAPER

Heavy, good quality drawing paper (cartridge paper, for example) is ideal to draw on. Watercolor paper is absorbent, often textured and is good for wet media or a drawing style that requires heavy texturing. Specialist drawing papers should be acid free, have good longevity and be resistant to discoloration. Construction paper (or sugar paper) is cheaper and grainier than drawing paper, is often colored and will age badly. Plain newsprint or lining paper (wallpaper) can be used if you need to economize but will discolor, and become yellow and brittle over time.

COLOR AND TONE

Bleached white paper is the most common, but off-white, ivory or buff is preferable for drawing on; it will show off drawn marks more sympathetically and can be heightened with white. You can use colored papers but if you do, test how the medium looks on it first.

WEIGHT

Weight of paper is measured in pounds per ream (poundage or lb.) or in grams per square meter (gsm). Papers between 65–135 lb. (100–200 gsm) are good for drawing on. The paper's weight affects the feel of the mark on the page although weight doesn't always relate to quality—for example you can get very lightweight Chinese and Japanese papers for specialist tasks.

SIZE

When you are choosing what size of paper to draw on think about practicality; small sketchbooks are good for taking out and about, whereas a static set up with an easel will allow you to use large paper. Also think about what kind of marks you want to make; small paper encourages short marks from the fingers and wrist and can be covered quickly; larger paper encourages sweeping marks from the shoulder and elbow.

Drawing Boards

You'll need a flat surface to rest your paper on, ideally
something you can hold at an angle and take around ·
with you while sketching. A rigid, lightweight piece of
board, slightly larger than your paper is ideal; pegs,
clips or masking tape will secure your paper in place.
If the plane of the paper is angled toward your face
it will be easier to make direct comparisons between
paper and model.

Working on a drawing board on an easel can help
with observational drawing, although it can give you
arm-ache if you're not used to it! Working flat on a table
increases the risk of distortions in the drawing and can
put strain on your back and neck.

Sketchbooks

Sketchbooks are practical and personal; they protect your paper, keep your work in order and small ones are easy to carry around. Ring-bound books can be folded back giving a flat plane of paper but the bindings can break if treated roughly. Hardback sketchbooks are naturally supported; softback books can be cheap but bend too easily. Always think about the type of paper in your sketchbook and find a size and dimension that suits your purposes. Loose paper can always be bound into a sketchbook later.

Graphite

PENCILS

For drawing, graphite (lead) pencils give smooth, gray marks with a slightly shiny surface. Graphite pencil is very adaptable, can be rubbed out cleanly, and gives a controlled line. Pencils have different grades, measured on a scale of 9H–9B with HB in the middle—H stands for hard and B for black.

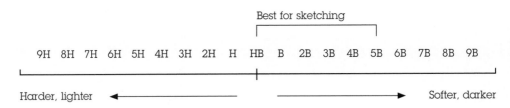

Best for sketching

| 9H | 8H | 7H | 6H | 5H | 4H | 3H | 2H | H | HB | B | 2B | 3B | 4B | 5B | 6B | 7B | 8B | 9B |

Harder, lighter ◄———————   ———————► Softer, darker

SHARPENING

Pencils should be kept sharp for consistent drawing. Sometimes you'll want a blunt pencil so that you can achieve a wider, softer line, in which case you can use sandpaper to wear one edge down.

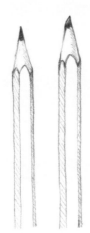

GRAPHITE POWDER

Avoid smudging pencil with your finger as it can be difficult to control; if you want to achieve soft tones you can buy powdered graphite that can be applied to your paper with a finger, paintbrush, stump or tortillion (blunt shaping tools made of rolled paper).

ERASERS

Putty erasers come in grades of softness. They are malleable, darken with use, and are best for rubbing out charcoal or graphite powder.

Plastic erasers come in various qualities with cheap not always meaning bad; test a few to see how cleanly they rub out. Cut your eraser to a point so that you can use it as a drawing tool and keep your eraser clean to avoid unwanted smudging.

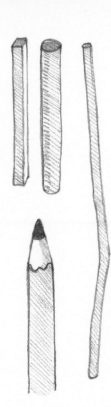

Charcoal

CHARCOAL
Charcoal is black and gives a varied, expressive line. The medium wants to smudge, and can be rubbed back with the hand and drawn into with an eraser to create light. Because of the difference in the quality of their surfaces, charcoal and graphite don't always mix well.

WILLOW
Willow charcoal comes in irregularly-sized sticks. It snaps easily and can be used on its side, point down or crushed and applied as powder.

COMPRESSED
Compressed charcoal is a dense black medium bound with gum arabic; it comes in uniform sticks, is harder to smudge, and doesn't rub out easily. Conté crayon, made from compressed charcoal and a clay or wax, is a good alternative with similar qualities.

PENCIL
Charcoal pencils are made from compressed charcoal in a pencil casing. They come in different grades of light, medium, and dark and give greater control over line than other charcoals.

Pen and Ink
Most ink pens cannot be erased, but do give clean lines, encouraging bold decisions in drawings and are a good choice for linear mark-making. Water-soluble ink can be wetted with a brush and used for painting in tone. All sorts of drawing tools (including brushes, bamboo, straws, etc.) can be dipped into pots of ink and drawn with. Ballpoint pens are cheap, versatile, and give a varied width of line. Fineliner pens provide a constant weight of line with better quality ink than ballpoints. Brush pens give a varying weight of line and are tricky to handle but with experience can be very expressive.

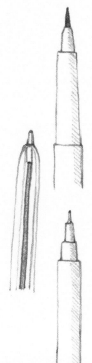

Who, Where, and When to Draw

Sketching Out and About

Once you have your materials you'll need people to
draw. Fortunately they're everywhere! Make it easy for
yourself to fit drawing into your day-to-day life: carry
a pocket sketchbook with you wherever you go and get
into the habit of making quick observational sketches
when you see somebody worth drawing. Here are
some tips designed to help you.

At Home

Set up facing the sofa. Anybody watching TV or falling
asleep will make a still and unsuspecting model.

Sketching in Cafés

Sitting by the window gives a range of views inside the café and out. If you're in a café opposite a bus stop your models will practically line up to be drawn.

Sketching on the Train

Sleepy commuters, partially glimpsed profiles and reflections in windows are all fair game for the guerilla draftsman.

Drawing from a Model

If covert outdoor sketching isn't your thing, or you want a model that isn't going to wander off halfway through your drawing, you might want to ask somebody to pose for you.

So You Need a Model

Firstly don't jump the gun; for your initial drawings you need someone who won't mind a few unflattering sketches being made of them! Here are a few ideas for finding people to draw.

- Learn to draw with somebody else. Take it in turn to pose for drawings; you can help one another progress and share tips and revelations. By posing for a drawing yourself you'll also learn to empathize with your own models.
- Find a friend or family member who doesn't mind sitting for a few first drawings. Exchanging the sittings for a meal, gardening, etc. can take away some of their expectation that you should create a good picture early on.
- Attend a life drawing class. Even if your aim isn't to draw nude figures you'll learn a lot from the process. It's a great opportunity to see the work of others and to share ideas.
- Once you're confident with your work, consider paying a professional artists' model to sit for you. You can often contact models via local art groups.

How to Run a Model Sitting

A session drawing from a model is called a "sitting" and the model a "sitter." Even when it is a very friendly and informal sitting there are a few things that are worth bearing in mind, particularly when drawing people who are not used to the experience.

- Firstly, be straight with your model about your level of experience: it will help you to throw yourself into the drawing without apprehension, keeping your drawings energetic and interesting.
- Set yourself an overall time limit for the session; an hour in total is often realistic, giving time for a chat, quick poses, a stretch, and a longer pose.
- Sit the model down comfortably and chat to them for a few minutes without drawing; explain what you'll be doing and that you need them to remain still, but that they can relax and find a comfortable position.
- Once you're ready to start, give your model somewhere to look. This will help them keep still. Put on some music to help you both relax.
- Make some quick drawings of five-minute poses to find a pose and composition you're happy with. These will get your eye and hand working together and will help you to learn the shape of your model's figure, clothes, and features.
- After several studies, have a break. Let the model stretch if they're feeling stiff from remaining still. Then try for a longer fifteen-minute picture; be strict with your timekeeping and know when to stop.
- Be honest with yourself about what the sitting is for. If it's a chance to sketch and chat keep it light and expect to make less considered drawings. If you're trying in earnest to learn and make better drawings you might want to cultivate a serious atmosphere. It's easy to get caught up in playing the artist; if you find yourself worrying about whether you look like a proper artist as you work then you're not paying enough attention to the model and your drawings will suffer for it. In the words of my own teacher John T. Freeman: "It should only be the model who is posing."

Life Studies vs. Photographs

This books mostly deals with drawing from life. When you're sketching from a real person you are translating something 3D (the model) into something 2D (your drawing) and you'll need to fully employ all of the skills of observational drawing. To capture the essence of your subject you want your drawing to be the result of a sitting where you can pick up on all of the characteristics that make your model unique, including all the little movements and shifts that can often be a source of frustration to the draftsman. Equally, if you're out and about sketching you want the hustle and bustle of the world around you to come through in the spontaneous and energetic marks of your drawings, mistakes and all!

Advantages of Drawing from Life
- Life sketches have a natural energy to them
- Your time is limited; you'll practice making intelligent, intuitive decisions
- Sketching from life is sociable and allows you to capture the feel of a situation or person

Disadvantages of Drawing from Life
- Life sketches are often incomplete
- Moving figures are hard to capture, and your model might have expectations of how your drawing will come out

Drawing from a Photo
A photo distances you from the subject of the picture and your drawing becomes a monolog of marks rather than a visual communication between model and draftsman. Translating a 2D image into another 2D image won't provide the opportunity to practice a full range of figure drawing skills, although it can allow you to draw figures without needing a model and in poses a model wouldn't be able to hold. There's no need to be snobbish about working from photos, as they can be a valuable source of imagery to draw from.

Advantages of Drawing from Photos

- You can go into greater detail drawing surface textures and clothing
- Folds in clothing and flows of hair remain in the same position
- You can draw poses that only occur fleetingly in life

Disadvantages of Drawing from Photos

- You are confined to working from only one angle and a single image
- Sketching from photos is solitary work
- As you have unlimited time, its very easy to overwork a picture and make it feel static and lifeless

It's very hard to make a good drawing from a poor photo, so work from the best possible imagery. Try to take your own photos for reference, making it easier to get the angles and lighting you want. Here is the setup that I use when drawing from photographs.

ABOUT DRAWING

Attitudes and Techniques

This chapter focuses on ways to think about drawing, complementing practice with a little theory to help you understand the revelations of drawing. As you do it more often, you'll come to realize that drawing isn't just about making pictures, it's about learning to see the world differently.

Attitudes are ways of thinking about and approaching the practice of drawing. The attitude you take to making a drawing is as important as the techniques you use to realize it. Techniques, such as the ones in this book, give you a starting point and a process to work through when translating your observation of the three-dimensional world into a two-dimensional drawing. Take all techniques with a pinch of salt. There is no right or wrong way to draw, just better and worse ways of achieving a certain outcome, or learning a particular way of seeing. Some techniques help you structure your time, the way you think about your subject, and the way you make your drawing; others provide clever tricks to make your drawing more striking. Use and adapt the techniques suggested here, combine them with other things you've read or been shown by fellow artists, discarding any approaches that don't suit you, and bring in your own understanding of the world. Do this, and given time you can be sure of developing an approach to drawing that is robust, authentic, and your very own.

Expectation and Intention

Rather than having expectations about the outcome of your drawing, aim to maintain integrity in your process. If you're making an observational study of a person, make sure that you really look at them closely, and that each mark you make on paper is the result of a clear observation. Every drawing you produce should be made for a reason; it is important to know why you are making a drawing before you do, even if that decision happens moments before your pencil touches the paper.

When you draw, you are selecting elements of another person that you've found interesting to reveal to a viewer through drawn marks. You might draw a person because you find their face interesting, in which case let your drawing dwell on their features. You might draw somebody to capture their gestures, or to record the clothes they are wearing, in which case make quick studies that capture their movements, or sketch the flow of fabric and the cut of their costume. First look, then formulate an intention; then draw with that in mind and don't waste time on elements of the figure that don't serve the intention of the drawing.

Risk and Failure

Failure is an integral part of learning. Every successful drawing a person makes is the tip of an iceberg of poorer drawings. It's important to maintain confidence when drawings fail and work out how to learn from a drawing that does not work in the way you would have liked. See all the drawings you make as part of a wider practice; every now and again you'll produce successful drawings. Most, however, most will simply be learning opportunities. Always be prepared to take risks in your work.

Style

Style is an elusive thing. Given the same medium and model we will all create different drawings with unique marks and emphasis. It is often only possible to understand your own style by going back over a body of old drawings to discover patterns in your work. Study the drawings of artists you respect, and of friends who draw. Learn lessons from their work by looking at how they have solved particular visual problems, what kind of marks they have made and what they are trying to say about their subject. Avoid simply copying, but use their drawings as a key to understanding how to improve your own. Don't worry about your personal style, it will develop over time and you'll often only recognize it retrospectively.

Core Skills of Drawing

Learn to Stare

Before looking at the perceptual skills of drawing it's worth thinking about what you are drawing from. We normally draw from three sources of imagery:

Observation: Directly looking at your subject, either from life or from secondary material.

Memory: Based on what we've memorized.

Imagination: Based on our ideas about how things might look or what we might like or expect to see, often relating to symbolic ways of thinking about the world.

It's important to recognize that all of these overlap. Even when you are drawing from observation you are having to remember things about your subject (when you look down at your paper to make a mark you're using your visual memory to hold the observation in your head) and your imagination (often in how you design the picture) to help you simplify the image. Equally, when you draw from imagination you're basing your imagined idea of a person on everything you remember about all the people, or representations of people, that you've ever seen. Observational drawing will help you improve your visual memory and broaden the bank of images that you use for imaginative drawing.

Observation   Memory   Imagination

Perceptual Skills

Perceptual skills are what we all use to take the very complex visual world and break it down into manageable elements that can be drawn. I'll relate all of these skills to the tutorials later—they are something to think about but it's not necessary to understand them all. The more you draw, the more they should make sense to you.

Seeing edges: Seeing boundaries, or outlines, often relates to linear drawing.

Seeing relationships: Identifying landmarks on a figure and relating these to one another, relates to the structure underneath a drawing.

Seeing shapes: Seeing spaces, shapes, blocks of tone or color, often relates to shapes of shadow on the figure.

Seeing tone: Highlight/shadow, light/dark, perceiving and comparing different values of black/gray/white.

Seeing the whole: Seeing a figure holistically, or as one thing. This is most difficult skill to grasp for beginners and builds naturally with the other skills.

Edges   Relationships   Shapes   Tone   Whole

Visual Language

The moment that pencil touches paper all of our perceptual skills come into play, all at once. It's important to understand that none of these processes (having an intention for your drawing, looking at your subject, perceiving the elements you wish to draw and making marks) are separate things. Drawing is a holistic skill and the mark-making happens while you are using your perceptual skills to understand the things that you're observing, remembering or imagining.

Making Marks

Drawing is a visual language that can directly describe the visual world. The marks we use in a drawing are equivalent to the words we use in written language. Scribbles, lines, dots, etc. all provide information about the subject they seek to describe and help to create an illusion of that subject on the page. Develop a more complex vocabulary of marks through experimentation, imitation, and practice (see Mark-Making, page 32).

Selective mark-making makes for a coherent drawing. Most beginners' drawings contain too many marks, laid down in a panic. You should never be afraid to make a mark but when you do, each should be the result of clear intent. The skill is in learning to make considered marks intuitively. If you can describe something in one line, don't go back over it three times. If you can describe something in 100 lines, don't put down 300.

Too many confused marks   Clarity of line

Picking the Right Vocabulary

Just as some occupations carry with them their own verbal language (anatomical or medical language used by doctors, engineers talking in terms of forces and materials, etc.) so different kinds of drawing require different visual vocabularies.

If the intention of a drawing is to study how a crowd looks en masse then shape and tone might be key to the drawing, and blocks of tonal mark-making might be the most appropriate vocabulary of marks to use.

If you're studying patterns on a dress, perhaps a linear vocabulary of marks might work best.

BUILDING SKILLS

Beginning and Improving

This chapter is all about improving your drawings.
If you're a total beginner, work your way through one
exercise at a time to build a foundation of understanding.
If you have some drawing experience, use and adapt the
exercises below to hone specific perceptual skills. You'll
learn the most by actually doing: draw, draw, draw, and
occasionally read something to help you solve a particular
problem. Most drawing tuition can be reduced to this:

- Look more closely at your subject.
- Make selective marks with greater clarity and intention.

Improving and Advancing

When you start drawing, the revelations come thick
and fast and improvements are often quick and easy to
recognize. As you become more experienced the leaps
forward are fewer and further between: little insights that
help you draw slightly better. No matter how good you
become you will always have days where you make
dreadful drawings, so don't expect each drawing to be
better than the last. Use your average work to measure
your progress rather than your best and worst work: make
many, many drawings, and look back over them after
some time to get a perspective on your own development.

Practice alone doesn't make for improvement; seek the
opinions of peers and teachers to help identify the strengths
and weaknesses in your drawings so that you can improve
on them. You may learn different techniques from different
people and some approaches may seem contradictory:
try everything, but stay true to your own intentions.
Learning to become a better draftsman is a life-long
journey and you'll find that you can assimilate many
different techniques into your own way of working.

Internal Tutor vs. Internal Critic

When you begin drawing your progress is hampered by a niggling internal monolog, saying things like: "I can't draw faces," "That leg can't possibly look like that," "This drawing isn't going very well." That's your internal critic, and it can be more restricting than any lack of ability. To develop, you need time to learn and draw without negative internal criticism, so instead nurture an internal tutor. Turn your inner criticisms into constructive questions that you can then try to answer in your drawings: "How much higher is the right eyebrow than the left eyebrow?" "Is that leg foreshortened? How can I make sense of its shape?" "What are the problems in this drawing that make it look unlike the subject? How can I improve on it?" Allow yourself time to step back from your drawing to ask these questions, and when you are drawing allow yourself to become absorbed in the process of looking and mark-making without criticism. It takes time to learn how to critique your own drawings constructively but it will come with practice.

Most importantly of all, enjoy making drawings. Drawing can be frustrating at times and as you improve, your goals will continue to recede away from you. There are myriad subjects, techniques, and mediums to learn about and you'll never get as good as you'll want to be, so take pleasure in the process of learning.

Seeing Tools

Looking

First look, then draw. Too often the beginner rushes to make marks before properly observing the person they are drawing. Do everything you can to make it easy to observe your subject; make sure you're comfortable and have your materials to hand, and ensure you have as good a light as possible on your model and paper.

Your eye is your most valuable drawing tool. With training, you can learn to accurately judge tones, angles and distances by eye, so practice making your measurements intuitively before resorting to using tools like plumb lines etc. Your aim as you draw is to establish a connection between your eye and your hand that circumnavigates the intellect, creating a state of flow in your process. You want to look, and to make marks in response to what you've seen without having to consciously think about where to put those marks. Your eyes should be constantly flitting from model to paper, paper to model, keeping the dialog between subject and paper fresh and immediate.

Seeing and Knowing

When you start drawing, you are unfamiliar with the visual world; just because we spend all day with our eyes open doesn't mean we know how to look. By learning to draw we learn to see again. Part of the learning process involves breaking down our ideas of how the world looks so that we can actually draw what we see in front of us. First, you should learn to become simply an eye that draws without thinking or rationalizing. As you look and draw more you start to rebuild your knowledge of the visual world to reflect what you've really observed. This is when thinking becomes helpful again. You'll become aware of the anatomy of the body, common shapes in the figure, the behavior of the figure in perspective, and of visual distortions like foreshortening. However you develop you want to begin with just seeing.

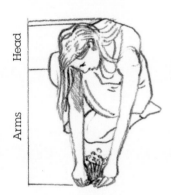

Head

Arms

Head

Arms

Visual Naivety

Your brain often stands in the way of clear observation, interpreting visual information in front of you as you try to draw so that you find yourself thinking things like: "An arm shouldn't be that long, maybe I haven't drawn it right." You should trust your eyes; what you see is what is true for your drawing.

Here's an example—in a body we think of the head as being above the shoulders and the arms being less than half of a person's height. In the drawing to the left this is true. In the drawing beneath it, the head is below the shoulders and the arms are the length of the whole figure; that is what you'd observe, that is what is true for this pose, so that is what you'd draw.

Thinking and Readjustment Lines

As you are learning to see, to judge your subject by eye and then to draw you'll sometimes find your marks going in places you don't want them to go. To find the "right" line in a drawing you'll often need to work through several "wrong" lines first. When you're not happy with the position of a line and you want to re-draw it elsewhere you might find it helpful to leave the incorrect line in: it stops you making the same mistake twice. Once you've re-drawn the line with more emphasis you can either erase the incorrect one, or leave it in. Those wrong lines can contribute something positive to the feeling of a drawing. They act as signposts to direct you to the right line and they provide insight into your process and can add dynamism to a drawing.

Sometimes you might find it helpful to use quick, light lines in-between your final marks to help you map out your observations on the page. These little "thinking lines" can help you get a feel for underlying shapes in the figure, particularly in quick sketches that don't allow enough time for underlying construction.

31

Mark-Making

The marks you make are your way of communicating with the future viewer of a drawing and are your way of describing and recording your subject. To help you think about mark-making, have a look back at the notes on visual vocabulary on page 26.

What You Are Drawing

When working on white paper with a dark pencil you are making dark marks on a light surface, so you want to look for dark shapes to draw. The marks also have a role as a metaphorical device. As well as communicating something about shape and outline, they can create an impression of texture, plunge part of the picture into darkness with tonal mark-making, and give the impression of speed and urgency or consideration and slowness. Think of words that might describe the surface of the part of the person you are drawing and then think of the kind of marks that fit those words.

For example, to the right, hairstyles: smooth, curly, wavy.

The marks you make feed into the intangible style of your drawings—they are your handwriting and how you make them will be individual to you. This isn't something you need to worry about; your way of making marks will develop over time. Try borrowing marks from other artists— Degas, Dürer, or Van Gogh, say; copy their lines to see how you like them and then develop your own through experimentation.

Making marks is a physical thing. Marks that come from the finger and thumb are short and quick. Marks made from the shoulder can be sweeping and wild and require big paper. As you make a mark think about where in your body you are drawing from.

Short marks from
thumb and forefinger

Long, arcing marks
from the wrist

Longer, sweeping
marks from the elbow

Think about how you hold your pencil as you make
a mark and explore different holding positions:

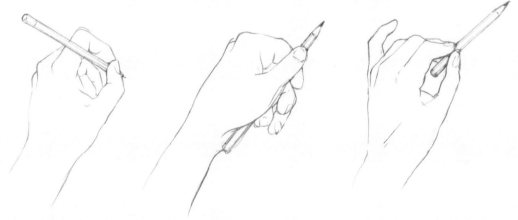

Controlling the point   Dragging a line   Using the side of the lead

Think about the speed of your marks as you draw
them—a quick line has flow and confidence, a slow
line has consistent weight (thickness), and a line
lifted from the paper has a directional quality.

Exercise: Eloquent Scribbles

What you need:

🕐 5 minutes

AIM

This exercise will help you explore mark-making. It is always helpful to do 30 seconds of practice mark-making before starting drawing to get your hand warmed up. You can take this further by exploring the mark-making of different artists.

METHOD: A LINE

Practice drawing a line. It seems basic, but it's well worth 30 seconds. Quickly make two dots on the paper and without thinking or hesitating, then join them with a line. Dot, dot, line. Repeat it and improve on it. Explore line weight by pressing hard, then lighter.

METHOD: TONE SHAPE

Find the easiest, clearest or most pleasing way to make a simple shape darker. Draw some little boxes, and fill them with marks. Firstly try straight, parallel diagonals, verticals and horizontals. Then try different kinds of cross-hatching. See how quickly you can fill the space. Try to stay within the lines, then allow yourself to go outside of the lines.

Use an eraser to bring in light, or to clean up the outside of the box.

Now use those marks to draw a cube; use thumb and finger marks, keep it small and quick:

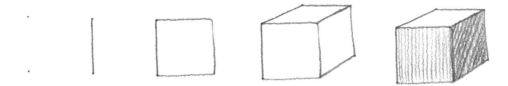

Edges and Lines

Most drawings begin with a line. A line can be a lasso, thrown around an idea or observation in order to give it initial form. Your first lines help map out your later intentions, giving you a simple visual framework that can be easily erased and shifted as your drawing develops.

We see the world tonally, in terms of light and dark. A line is an imposed idea that we use to simplify our observations of complex tones. It can help us select features that we consider important and separate an area of light from an area of dark, or an object from its environment.

Edges

To know where to draw a line you'll need to learn to perceive edges and make decisions about where the line should be drawn to represent that edge. Sometimes this can be obvious: if you have a dark object on a light background there is a clear tonal and literal edge to the object. Sometimes it is a judgment call you need to make—if there is a gradient of tone, at what point do you draw the line to separate the light area from the dark?

Tonal shape

See, Hold, Draw

When drawing from observation you look for an edge, perceive the line in it and hold the shape of that line in your head for a split second as you transfer it to paper. Be aware of that as you draw—you are seeing a line, holding it in your head, and then drawing it. Then you're looking for the next line.

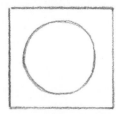

Outline

Object Boundaries

The first drawing top right ("Tonal shape") shows a dark shape and a light space; there is no actual line between the two, just an edge between tonally contrasting areas. The boundary between these areas of light and dark tone can be described by a single line ("Outline").

On the left side of the third drawing from top ("Light/dark") you see a light background and dark shape, while on the right you see a dark background and light shape. This contrast gives the illusion of three-dimensional form.

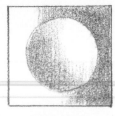

Light/dark

Edge of a Tonal Shape

This arm shows a gradient of tone across it. As well as having its own object boundary, the arm has shapes of tone within it that in turn have their own edges. When you draw these shapes you might find it helpful to start with a line around them, even if that line disappears into the tone later. You'll need to make a decision about exactly where you put that line—it's down to your judgment.

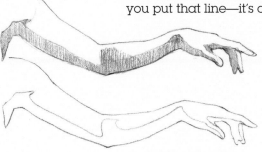

A Line for a Line

Sometimes a long, thin shadow creates a perceived line on the figure. A drawn mark can represent that line simply and directly. Look at whether the shadow varies in thickness and think about the weight of line, how heavily you press your pencil on the paper to replicate it, and if that pressure should vary.

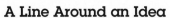

A Line Around an Idea

A line doesn't always have to be tied down by tonal representation. It can also help to reinforce an idea in a drawing. You can use lines to hint at what is below the surface of your subject, skirting around the shape of the figure under clothes, around muscular and skeletal shapes below the skin or suggesting the curvature of a surface by contouring over it.

Exercise: Blind Contour Drawing

What you need:

🕐 15 minutes

Aim

This exercise will help you make clear observations, unrestricted by worry about how the drawing looks. It will also help you to see edges and make decisions about where to draw a line. Finally, it encourages confident linear mark-making.

Method

Secure your paper and sit facing your subject. Set a timer for 3–10 minutes as you prefer, or put on music and draw for the length of a song. Touch your pencil to the paper, near the top and focus your eyes on the top of your model's head (your head if drawing in the mirror, or your object if working from a still life). Don't look down at your paper. Slowly, let your eye trace a line over your subject; as your eye "draws" its way across the surface of the subject let your pencil follow the same movements on the paper.

Draw in a continuous mark around your subject's outline, moving inwards to play over surfaces, shapes, and shadows. If you lose your place you may look down at your drawing once, reposition your pencil, and continue the process again, keeping your eye on the subject while drawing at the same time.

As you draw, think about what kind of edges you are seeing and drawing. Is your line moving over an object boundary? Is it defining a boundary between light and dark? Are you contouring over the surface of skin?

Expect the drawing to appear bizarre and disproportioned; after all, you weren't looking at it! Repeat regularly to help you get used to looking and drawing.

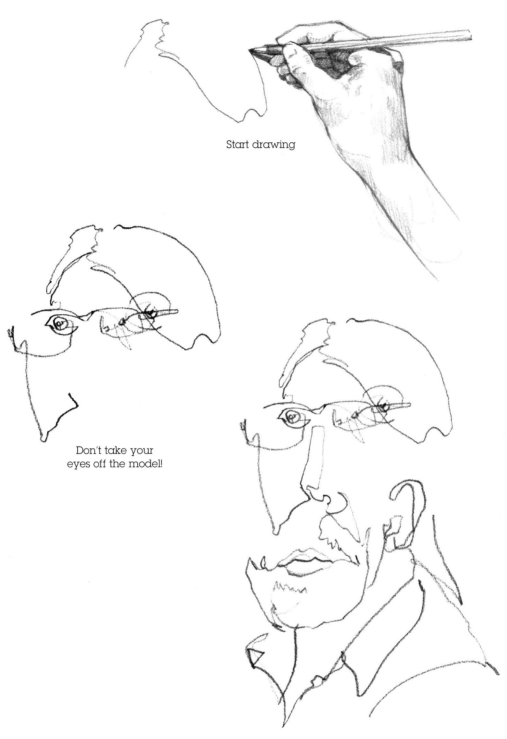

Start drawing

Don't take your
eyes off the model!

The finished drawing

Relationships and Points

A drawing is made up of marks arranged on a page. It is important to develop an understanding of how shapes and points sit together in context with one another to reflect the relationships you perceive in your subject. Problems proportioning the figure usually derive from mistakes made perceiving the relationships between one part of the body and another. The more time you spend looking for and isolating landmarks the easier you will find them.

A Bridge Between Points

As well as having its own intrinsic qualities of rhythm and weight, a line bridges a gap between two points—it has a beginning and an end. Judge what kind of line is needed to bridge the gap between two points. You might make a convex or concave line; it could be made slowly or quickly; it could run straight or curve back on itself. Look at where the line will start and end before you make the mark.

Landmarks   Relationship between landmarks

Relationships Between Shapes

As well as looking for relationships between points you can relate one shape to another across a figure. It is often helpful to look at the broad relationships between shapes of a similar kind; for example, you could look at how all of the midtone shapes of shadow are positioned on a figure and try to perceive their relationships— is one shape at a diagonal to the other shape, or are they horizontally aligned? You might also look for relationships between landmarks—is one knee higher than the other knee? Think of these groups of shapes like constellations of stars on the figure.

Midtone shadow shapes   Dark shadow shapes

Outline
tangents

Developed
tangents

Vertical:
forehead,
chest, knee

Horizontal:
chin,
shoulder

Distant
relationship

Close
relationship

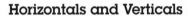

Tangents

The human figure is bound by convex or concave lines joined together in flows. Rather than get caught up in the undulations of the figure it can sometimes be helpful to look at the average line of a curve in order to simplify a shape. This might mean looking for a tangent that touches the edge of a curve, or a line that cuts through a curve, traveling between two points. Imagine you are a sculptor cutting away at a block of marble. To find the figure underneath you have to "rough out" the general form.

Horizontals and Verticals

Vertical and horizontal relationships can be the easiest relationships to judge. When you place a new mark check if it should be above, below, to the left or right of other marks you have drawn.

Close and Distant Relationships

When you place a new mark on your drawing, you tend to think about how it relates to close neighboring marks. Simultaneously consider how it relates to more distant points. This will help the drawing develop as a whole, rather than in disparate parts. It might be helpful to have a single point, established early, that you refer back to every time you place a new mark.

Exercise: Sight-Size Portrait

What you need:

🕐 15 minutes or more

Aim

This exercise will help you identify and compare points in the face and will encourage you to check relationships between shapes.

Method

Sit so that you can see your paper and the model at once; your easel will hold the paper in the plane of your model's face and the lamp ensures consistent shadows. A sight-size drawing is made the same size as you see it, with measurements taken directly from the subject. It is important to maintain a constant viewing position to stop your view of the model shifting.

Line up your pencil with the top of the model's head, trace your eye along it and fix a point on the paper, then mark the paper exactly where you are looking. Do the same for the chin. Work your way through the face in this way, finding a point, lining it up with the model at the scale you are seeing them and mark that point on the paper. Use measuring techniques from the end of this chapter to help you.

Constantly look from model to drawing. Draw exactly and only what you see and be strict with yourself; if the mark doesn't line up, alter it. At first you'll have a blank page speckled with points but as you continue you'll find you can join those points with lines and blocks of shadow.

The sight-size technique is often used in time consuming drawings and paintings; adjust the exercise to suit your purpose.

Setup

Draw the size you see the object

First marks

Shadow shapes

Tone

Shapes and Spaces

As soon as you make two marks on the page you create
a space between those marks. Seeing shapes in the figure
is about simplifying something complex. A person can be
simplified into an arrangement of geometric shapes and
a complex gradient of shadow can be broken down into
simple shapes of different tones. A shape is a set of points
joined by lines to give it edges, so seeing and drawing
a shape relates to previous perceptual skills. Two kinds
of shape are particularly useful in drawing people—
underlying shapes for constructing the figure and tonal
shapes for the surface of the figure.

Underlying Shapes

You can use the "idea" of a shape to underpin general
forms in the figure. Imagine you are making the figure
from clay—first you might build up big blocks to establish
a general shape before defining the curves of the body.
As you look for these underlying shapes think in metaphors.
Is the pose spire like and triangular? Is it square? Is the
figure curled into a ball?

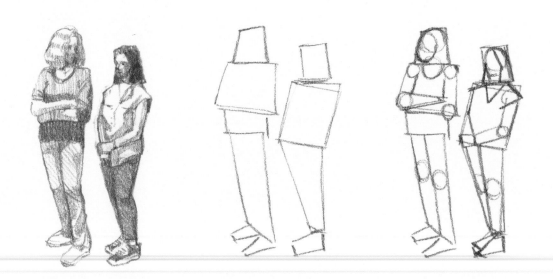

Tonal Shapes

Tonal shapes are the simplified shapes of shadow and highlight by which we perceive the surface of the figure. When you're drawing with a dark medium on a light surface you tend to look for shapes of shadow, because it is the dark shadow you'll actually draw. Maintain an awareness of the highlight shapes at the same time. All the shapes should fit together to make a visual jigsaw. All you should need to do is to draw each shape as you see them, in the correct tone and the correct place.

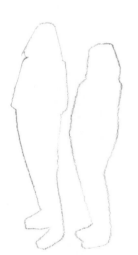

Big Shapes to Smaller Shapes

Whether you're drawing underlying or surface shapes, you want to look for big shapes first, then smaller shapes.

Exercise: Tiny People

What you need:

🕐 15 minutes

Aim

To teach you to look for shapes in figures, freeing yourself
up from concentrating on detail.

Method

Sit outside a café looking down a street or into the park,
anywhere where people are likely to be still or walking
slowly. You'll need plenty of distance between you and
the figures you are drawing, or have a few photographs
that show whole figures.

Fill a page with small drawings of people, no larger
than your little finger, scattered around the page. Avoid
detail and draw them as if you were carving them from
wood. Jot a mark for the top, bottom, left and right of the
figure. Find the middle of the figure to give you some
points to navigate by.

Look for simple shapes in and around the body. Draw
them quickly as blocks, spending no more than a minute
on each and using your thumb and forefinger to make
swift, neat marks.

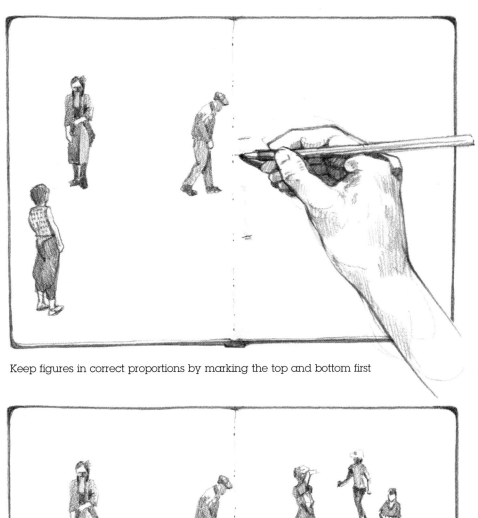

Keep figures in correct proportions by marking the top and bottom first

Keep filling a page, the figures don't need to relate to one another

Light and Tone

We see the world by perceiving light. Everything we see can be understood as having color and tone. We think of color in terms of a rainbow spectrum—red, yellow, etc., but in a monochrome drawing everything needs to be simplified to tonal values. Think of tone as the grayscale in a black-and-white photograph. It is not the same as color, although colors have tone. Practice recognizing the tones of colors by imagining them being photocopied in black-and-white. Tone is also called "value," and tone in a drawing is often referred to as "shading."

The light that falls on figures sculpts the shadows on them; the shadow is created by the interruption of light by a form. While line is an imposed idea used to simplify an edge, tonal drawing reflects how we actually see the world by using a map of shading to create a direct illusion of what we see. Tone can be used selectively to give drawn surfaces curvature and figures a sense of three-dimensional form.

Recognizing Relative Tones

Tone is seen as a gradient, merging from light to dark. To represent these shadows you'll need to simplify them. Train yourself to look for dark mid-tones, mid-tones, and light mid-tones and practice mark-making techniques for those different bands of tone so that you become better at looking and identifying them and being able to draw them quickly and clearly. Beginners tend to make overly dark shadows; the visual world is mostly mid-tone punctuated by relative darks and lights.

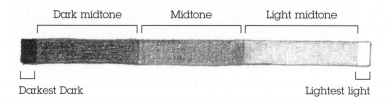

Dark midtone   Midtone   Light midtone

Darkest Dark   Lightest light

Tonal Range

The materials you use set the potential tonal range in your drawing. The darkest tone you'll be able to achieve is at one end of the scale and is made by pressing the pencil hard against the page. The lightest tone is the white of the paper and sits at the other end of the scale. Different grades of pencil will give different tonal ranges with darker Bs giving a wider total range and lighter Hs a more subtle, narrow tonal rage.

Tonal gradients made with the tip and side of a pencil.

Start with several grades of pencil and experiment with them to work out their ranges and which grades you prefer.

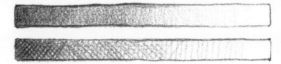

HB

2B

5B

To get the widest range and subtlety, try using three pencils.

| 5B | 2B | HB | HB + eraser |

Light source

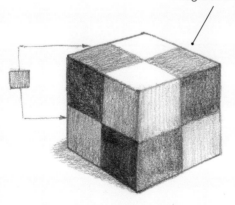

Illusion

On this cube the dark square on the light side is exactly the same tone as the light square on the dark side. Our eyes see the tone, and our brains interpret it as a lighting effect by contextualizing it against its surroundings. Be aware of this illusion as you are drawing, and practice recognizing tones on their own to make them easier to replicate.

Exercise: Subtractive Tone

What you need:

🕐 15 minutes

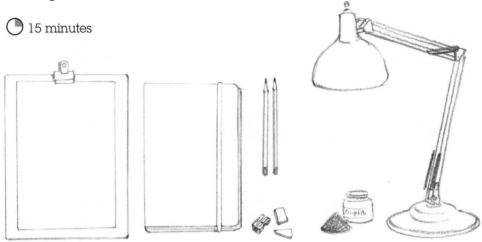

Aim

The aim of this exercise is to help you recognize and draw shapes of tone.

Method

Light your model with the lamp to create defined tones to draw. Prepare your paper by lightly rubbing graphite powder into it with a cloth. Don't scrub it in too hard but aim to cover the surface with a mid-tone of grey. This also works well with charcoal.

Take a good plastic eraser, cut to a point, and start drawing in shapes of light. Start from a clear shape of highlight and erase areas of light as you see them, keeping aware of the relationships between shapes. Try to match the tone of the drawing to what you see. You are just looking to differentiate shapes of shadow from shapes of highlight.

Once you have drawn in as much of the light as you can, look for darker darks, using your pencil to add shadows back into the picture. Work backwards and forwards, adding dark and subtracting light until your time is up.

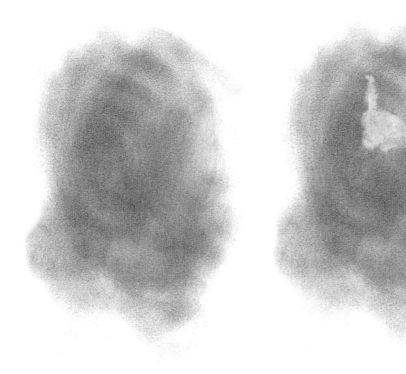

Graphite powder on paper

Draw light with eraser

Find highlight shapes

Shadows added with pencil

Seeing People as a Whole

An awareness of "the whole" is the most difficult perceptual skill to explain. It generally develops as your drawing improves. Essentially, it is important to be aware of the figure as a whole, even as you draw the smaller components that make up the body. As you look and draw, you want to zoom into specific details to tap into the finer proportions of the figure, and then to zoom out again to appreciate the overall form.

If you only work from one part of the body to another you tend to slip out of proportion over the course of the whole drawing, so that by the end you may have lost the top of the head off the page, feet off the bottom, or have the head fall out of proportion with the torso. If you notice something going wrong correct it immediately; it is better to establish good habits than to preserve disparate elements of the drawing. It is always okay to allow a drawing to distort if that is your intention but remember that stylization isn't the same as incompetence.

Objective Analysis

In order to see your drawing more objectively and make decisions about how to improve it, try looking at it upside down, in a mirror, or look at a photograph of your drawing. Distance will always help. Step back from your drawing or hold it out at arm's length to get a better impression of the whole figure.

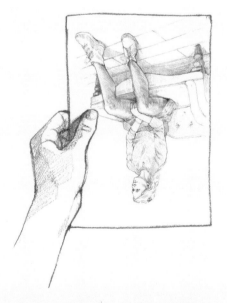

Observational Measuring

Although intuitive visual measuring is always the ideal, you'll find that at all stages in your drawing education there will be times when you can't quite judge a distance by eye. That is when you can introduce observational measuring tools to help you see and make accurate comparisons.

Measuring with a Pencil

Have you ever seen an artist squinting down their outstretched arm, pencil held up in front of them? This is what they are doing. Hold your pencil at arm's length (to keep the measurements consistent), close one eye (to flatten what you see) and put the top of the pencil against one edge of the subject you want to measure. Slide your thumb down the pencil to line up with the other end of your subject. You now have a distance that you can compare to other parts of the subject. This approach to measuring makes you look dreadfully artistic but don't get carried away; it is best to only use it for checking proportions you can't judge by eye. Here are some examples of how to use the measurements.

 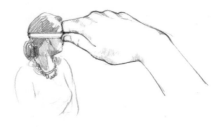

Comparing a length to a width

1

1

Working out how many of lengths fit into another length

Verticals, Horizontals, and Diagonals

You can use your pencil to check angles in your drawings and to establish horizontal and vertical relationships across a picture. A plumb line can be used for the same task.

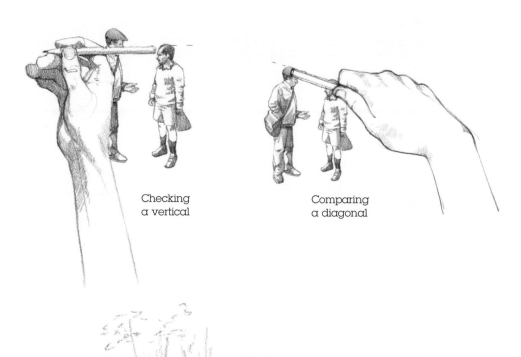

Checking
a vertical

Comparing
a diagonal

Figure in a Space

You can use the environment around a figure to measure against people's proportions, and use vertical or horizontal objects in the background to compare to your figures.

Establish, Construct, Elaborate

The Technique

This approach to observational drawing can be applied to any subject—the idea of the three broad stages is to give you time to draw one aspect of the subject at a time. Erasing between the stages is important, not to get rid of what you've done, but to "push back" your marks to make way for the next layer. By working in layers you'll be able to think about one problem at a time and then push the layer back, using the success of the under-drawing to aid your next layer while correcting any problems in the observation. It allows you to keep your marks fresh and to look your way through the whole subject several times while finishing one little section at a time.

At each stage you'll want to look for different aspects in the subject. This is explained in greater detail in the next chapter. Here's what you'll be looking for at the different stages.

Establish

You're aiming to make a quick, intuitive response to the subject. It is an opportunity to look your way through the whole subject without getting caught up in detail or careful proportioning. Look for flows, gestural lines, and big shapes. Keep your hand loose and draw quickly.

Construct

You're aiming to map out simple geometric shapes over the initial gestural establishing drawing. This is where you map out the proportions of your subject; as you find inaccuracies in your previous, partially-erased sketch, erase them further and draw over them. There are no right or wrong shapes to find; the more you look for underlying shapes the more you'll find them. Stay quick, draw lightly and confidently, and pay particular attention to the relationships between different parts of your subject.

Elaborate

Elaborating on the previous under-drawings means looking more at the surface, and putting down the final lines that will represent your subject. Remember the energetic marks of the establishing drawing and build on the accuracy of the constructed drawing. Trust the proportions of the past layers, but if you come across inaccuracies that you want to improve upon feel free to erase and redraw that area. It can help to first think about the line, looking for object outlines and shapes of shadows to draw down, working lightly at first. Then look for tone, thinking about separating shadows into light and dark mid-tones. Finally think about your darkest darks and lightest lights, using a darker pencil mark to selectively deepen shadows and using an eraser to tidy up edges and bring out highlights. You can take this stage as far as you like, but it's good to learn when to stop.

A Beginner's Approach

The first stage, establishing the shape, can be the most difficult for beginners as it relies on a certain level of understanding and draftsmanship. Although it is the ideal way to begin, and you shouldn't be afraid to try it, you might find it easier to start with the construction stage. As you advance as a draftsman, revisit these early instructions to see if you can gain a better appreciation of them with experience.

Exercise: Establish, Construct, Elaborate

What you need:

🕐 15 minutes

Aim
This exercise will familiarize you with the technique used in the next chapter.

Method
Put a hat (other objects will work just fine of course) down in front of you; make sure you are comfortable and that the hat and your paper are well lit.

Establish
Look at the hat. Get an impression of its shape, the character of line in its brim, and how light or dark it is. Looking mostly at the hat and occasionally glancing back at your drawing use a swift, continuous, gestural line to sketch its rough outline. Lightly erase the drawing to push the sketch into the background, leaving it visible so that it can be easily drawn over.

Construct
Using the establishing sketch as a rough guide, look for and draw any underlying shapes that underpin the form of the hat. Look for ovals and circles underneath its curves and use straight lines to simplify some if necessary. Lightly erase this layer as well.

Elaborate
Using the constructed shapes as a guide, draw the outline of the hat, thinking about how the weight of line should vary to give the drawing variety. Concentrate on the surface qualities of the hat, looking for blocks of tone to draw, and use efficient, clear mark-making to replicate textures and shadows. Finish by using an eraser to clean up stray lines and bring highlights back into the drawing.

1) Look

2) Establish

3) Erase

4) Construct

5) Elaborate on line

6) Elaborate on tone

THE 15-MINUTE FIGURE

The Basic Figure

This chapter focuses on using layered drawings to create a figure sketch in around fifteen minutes. The approach should ideally be practiced with a model posing for you, although it can be applied to working from secondary sources. Quick sketches of figures made on location will still utilize many of the methods explained in this chapter, but in those quicker drawings you won't have time to construct and elaborate in such a considered fashion.

Long, laborious drawing doesn't necessarily come out looking better than quick drawings; quick drawings can make for very engaging images. If you're clever with your drawn selections, the fewer marks you put down the more accurate a sketch can appear, as the viewer is left to fill in the gaps. The longer you spend on a drawing, the more accurate you have to be to make it convincing.

A Visual Conversation

When you draw somebody from life think of the process as similar to meeting them for the first time. At first you take in their overall shape and appearance, then you might engage with their eyes, finally your gaze might move around the rest of their face and their hands to take in their expression and gestures. By following a similar approach in your drawings (sketch a general impression, then hone in on features and details) you follow a familiar and rehearsed way of seeing people. It is important not to leave hands and faces out of a drawing unless you have a good reason to. The face and hands represent the essence of your model's identity; a figure without hands and face is just an anonymous, limbed torso. If you're afraid to approach any part of the figure use the tutorials later in the book to help you, and remember—just draw the shapes you see in front of you. By working visually you can break the figure down into a simple form of lines and shadows.

Focus

Focus in a drawing is important. You want to know what your drawing is about so that you can direct your process to best fulfill your intentions. You don't always have to draw a full figure. If you're drawing a portrait ask yourself: "Am I focusing on just the head, the head and shoulders, or the whole torso?" If you're drawing a full figure, is the focus on the figure in its environment, their clothing, their expression and gesture? Direct the time you spend on a drawing accordingly.

Face and hands

Time

The more you draw people the better you'll get at predicting how long it takes to make a drawing. Manage your time as you draw—if you have fifteen minutes, how long should you spend on each part? Perhaps five minutes sketching the whole figure in, then two minutes per hand, five minutes for the face, five minutes for the costume? It's up to you how you divide the time, just ensure it suits the intentions of your drawing.

Poor time management is often mistaken for poor drawing. For example, somebody might think they can't draw hands—in fact their problem isn't their drawing; it is that they always add hands in the last 30 seconds of the pose rather than making the time to properly study them. A little more time and some careful observation could solve this problem.

Costume focus

Figure in a room

Stage 1: Establish the Pose

What Is Establishing?

The establishing sketch is a fast, gestural drawing that helps you break the white of the paper and make a few beginning marks before committing to a more solid form. It is an excuse to look, forcing you to properly observe your subject. As you draw, make sure you look at the model more than you look at your paper. Establishing sets the scale of your drawing—it ensures you get a holistic impression of the pose and can stop you falling out of proportion as you draw. It can end with erasure, to prepare for the construction stage; or it can be a finished, gestural study in its own right.

What Skills Does It Use?

- The establishing sketch requires holistic observation of the pose; it is about seeing big shapes and outlines in the figure and jotting those shapes down straight from your eye.
- It particularly requires you to see the edges of shapes, shadows, and outlines in the figure.

◔ 10 seconds–1 minute

Mark-Making

Use swift, flowing lines.

How to Improve

Practice making quick, incomplete sketches from life; improvement will come with the development of your general drawing skills.

ESTABLISH

A: <u>GESTURAL SKETCH</u>

B: <u>ERASE</u>

Stage 2: Construct

What Is Constructing?
The construction drawing is a scaffold of shapes that underpins the body and clothing of the person you are drawing. Sometimes these shapes are purely visual—just what you see in the pose—and sometimes they relate to set landmarks in the body. This layer of drawing provides a structure on which to "hang" your observations of the figure's surface. I have broken down the construction stage into sub-stages: firstly, the drawing of simple shapes that identify the key masses and landmarks, and secondly, the drawing of tangents and flows which join these forms. As with the previous stages, the lines are laid down in order to be erased later—some draftsmen like the construction lines showing through to give a hint to the artist's process, where others prefer to get rid of them. As with all the instruction here, adapt it to your needs and preferences.

What Skills Does It Use?
- A knowledge of human anatomy and the behavior of fabric can help at this stage.
- It helps to be able to perceive the relationships between shapes, as well as seeing the shapes themselves.

◔ 3–5 minutes

Mark-Making
Loose circles and ovals joined by flowing lines for internal construction and quick, direct lines for tangents.

How to Improve
Study basic anatomy, draw draped fabric and practice looking for shapes within objects.

A: <u>BASIC INTERNAL SHAPES</u>

B: <u>FLOWS AND TANGENTS</u>

Parallel Stage: the Clothed Figure

What Is a Parallel Stage?

Parallel stages are more about understanding than drawing—as you construct the figure, it is helpful to be aware of certain features that are present in all clothed figures so that when you come across these in your drawing you aren't surprised by them. The construction stage of drawing reflects the drawn anatomy of a clothed figure, encompassing an awareness of where the body is beneath the clothes, the physical anatomy of that body and the behavior of clothing and fabric on the figure. You could think of tailors' patterns and the behavior of different fabrics as the "anatomy" of clothing.

Clothing on the Figure

Clothing has many purposes (see Chapter 6, page 104). Think about the shapes that clothes make on the body and how they divide up sections of the figure underneath them to make arms and hands, and heads and necks into their own little jigsaw-shapes. Notice the big shapes in flows of fabric and learn to recognize important folds, drawing these first before getting caught up in detailed textures. Some items of clothing flow with the shape of the figure, becoming like another layer of skin that mimics the body below. Others have unique shapes that they bring to the drawing, introducing new sculptural forms to the figure, often obscuring the body underneath. Bring an awareness of clothing to the construction stage as you look for large shapes.

How to Improve

- Draw from draped fabric to learn more about shapes in folds, and learn more about clothes patterns.
- Practice looking for the shapes of shadow that create the impression of folds.

Think about: clothing shapes

Think about: fabric folds

Parallel Stage: Anatomy

The Body

As well as learning to clearly see the shapes on the surface
of the figure, it's important to maintain an awareness of
the body's shape beneath the clothes. Knowledge of the
underlying figure can help you solve problems in your
drawing and will make it easier to identity the relationships
between important landmarks.

Anatomy

When your subject is wearing tight clothing, or has bare
arms, legs, etc., you will see something of the anatomy
of the body expressed on the surface of the skin; shadows
that hint at jutting edges of bone and flows of muscle
etc. An understanding of human anatomy can improve
your figure drawing, but it isn't an absolute necessity.
A broad knowledge of the skeleton can be valuable
for understanding the proportions of the figure and an
understanding of the behavior of muscles and fat can
be helpful.

Drawn Anatomy

The landmarks you look for in the construction stage
(joins, big bone masses, and important muscular flows)
are invariably related to key parts of a person's anatomy.
It can be helpful to develop a simplified drawn anatomy
that you can bring into a drawing when constructing
the figure.

How to Improve

- Attend life drawing classes to learn more about
  the figure.
- Use an artists' anatomy book to learn more about
  the anatomy of the body.

Think about: the body

Think about: drawn anatomy

Anatomy and Drawn Anatomy

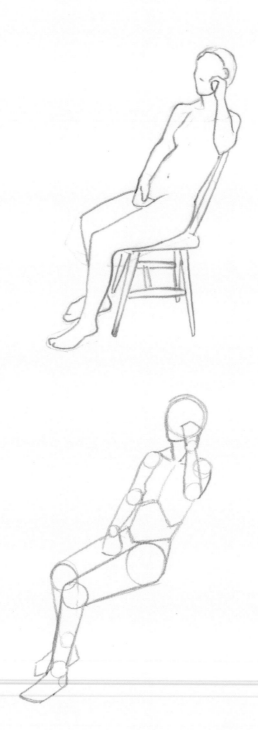

Think about: the skeleton

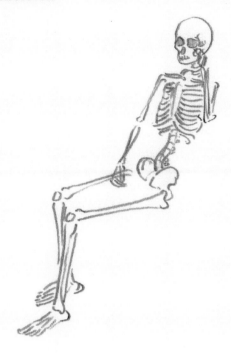

Think about: muscles

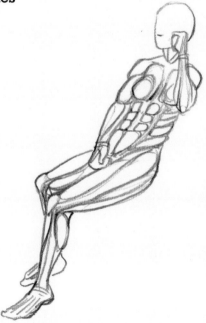

Negative Space

What Is Negative Space?

Negative spaces are the shapes around your subject that aren't a part of the subject itself—the spaces between limbs, or between a figure and its environment. When you think of your drawing as a jigsaw, you could imagine that as well as a person-shaped piece there are many negative space pieces that fit around the person to make up the rectangle of the paper. Seeing negative spaces around the figure will help you during the construction stage, particularly if you're having trouble working out how to draw a part of the body.

What Skills Does It Use?

The ability to recognize abstract shapes as well as perceiving the relationships between shapes.

 1–2 minutes

Mark-Making

Abstract shapes, often made from relatively straight lines.

How to Improve

Practice looking for negative spaces around and between objects—you can use a viewfinder (a piece of paper or card with a rectangle cut in the middle) to help you recognize shapes around the body.

CONSTRUCT (CONTINUED)

C: INTERNAL NEGATIVE SPACES

D: EXTERNAL NEGATIVE SPACES

Parallel Stage: Problem Solving

What Is Problem Solving?

If something doesn't look right in your drawing this is the best time to change it. Even if it means erasing most of what you have done to find the correct line it is important to get into good habits. You'll need your internal tutor here (page 29), as this is a good moment to hold your drawing out at arms length and compare it to your subject; does it feel right? Does anything need changing? What are the problems you can identity?

How to Check for a Problem

The most effective ways of checking for problems are ensuring that the negative spaces appear to be the correct shapes and checking the correct parts of the body line up with one another along vertical and horizontal lines (see page 41). Check the drawing against your subject, identify where any problems may be, erase those areas and re-draw them more accurately.

Look at: spaces and shapes

Look at: vertical and horizontals

Stage 3: Elaborate

What Does Elaborate Mean?

Elaborating on the drawing means drawing what you see on the surface of your model, the things you actually see. It includes the light and shadow on the surface of your subject and the actual outline of the figure. Work out what you want to include in the drawing, how much detail you want to go into and layer that over the top of your semi-erased construction drawing. This is the stage where you can exercise considerations of design, deciding what will look best where and whether you want to make the drawing tonally representative, or linear, or to stylize elements of it. As you build on the earlier layers with the final stages of drawing remember the energy of the first establishing sketch—the marks you make now should be better placed and more considered, but no less energetic.

What Skills Does It Use?

- You'll need to employ your skills of recognizing shapes for drawing shadows and comparison of tone for the light and dark.
- Decision-making and design play a large part that involves selection and imagination.

🕐 5–10 minutes

Mark-Making

You can bring the full range of your mark-making to bear on the surface, experiment with different kinds of linear and tonal mark-making in hair, skin and fabric. (See chapter 6 for more detail.)

How to Improve

Improving at this stage is partly about developing your own style of drawing—practice mark-making that you find pleasing and working out what it is you want to say in your drawings. One of the greatest skills is knowing when to stop.

A: ELABORATE ON LINE

B: ELABORATE ON TONE

C: LIGHTEST LIGHTS AND DARKEST DARKS

D: THE FIGURE'S ENVIRONMENT

THE FINISHED DRAWING

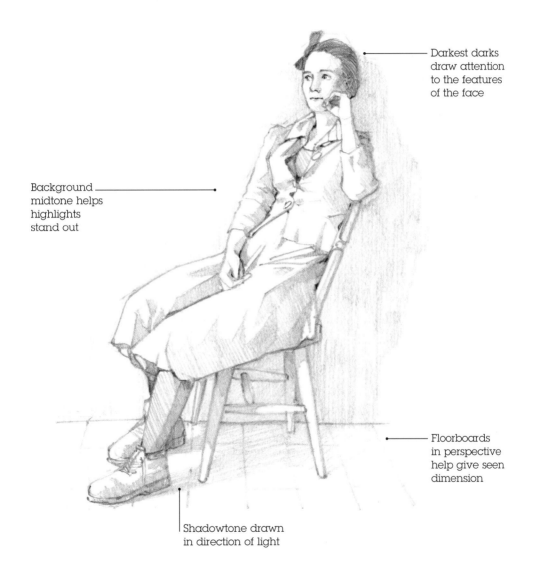

Darkest darks
draw attention
to the features
of the face

Background
midtone helps
highlights
stand out

Floorboards
in perspective
help give seen
dimension

Shadowtone drawn
in direction of light

Putting It All Together

Here is the whole process as a step-by-step drawing—
use it to refer to, then practice it yourself.

Remember to look!

STAGE 1

ESTABLISH

A: GESTURAL SKETCH

B: ERASE

STAGE 2

CONSTRUCT

A: BASIC INTERNAL SHAPES

Think about anatomy!

B: FLOWS BETWEEN SHAPES

C: INTERNAL NEGATIVE SPACES

D: EXTERNAL NEGATIVE SPACES

Problem-solve; check, erase, and redraw if needed!

E: ERASE

STAGE 3

ELABORATE

A: ELABORATE ON LINE

B: ELABORATE ON TONE

C: <u>LIGHTEST LIGHTS, DARKEST DARKS</u>

D: <u>ENVIRONMENT</u>

Exercise: a Person in 15 Minutes

What you need:

🕐 15 minutes

Aim

This exercise will help you get to grips with the process of establishing, constructing, and elaborating from a model.

Method

It shouldn't take more than fifteen minutes from setup to finish, but there's no harm in taking longer, so long as you set a time limit for yourself and stick to it (agree the time with your model first!). Aim to stick to the stages suggested rather than drawing as you might normally draw and work through each step, keeping an eye on the time as you do. Set yourself up comfortably before you begin, making sure you can see your model and paper without having to move your head too much. Decide at the beginning whether you're going to do a full figure study, a partial figure or a portrait, and stick to this intention.

A) Look

B) Stage 1: Establish

C) Erase

D) Stage 2: Construct

E) Erase

F) Stage 3: Elaborate

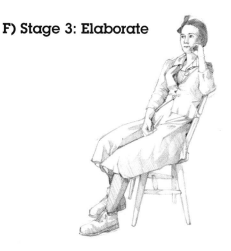

GOING INTO DETAIL

The Head

When you're drawing the figure, think of the head as an object. It is easy to get caught up in the details of the face but the face is a small part of the mass of the whole head: the neck, the hair, and the shape of the skull all contribute to our overall impression of the head.

If you're drawing the head as part of a fifteen-minute sketch you might have around five minutes to jot down its essential characteristics. See the short time frame as positive; it will make it easier to make quick, intuitive decisions. The fewer marks you make, the more the viewer's mind will fill in for; so long as your marks are made as the result of considered observation they stand a good chance of coming across well.

We often think of the face and head symbolically; we expect to see two eyes, one nose, one mouth, two ears. We have schemas, cartoon-like symbols, held in our minds to represent these elements. Free yourself from those expectations: see what is in front of you as a collection of shapes and shadows. Draw what you see

The Head as Part of the Figure

When you're drawing simple figures a simple depiction of the head will serve you just fine. Think about shop mannequins; the most basic mannequins indicate the head with a curved top of the skull, a jaw, and a neck to connect it to the body. That's all you need include on the most basic figure.

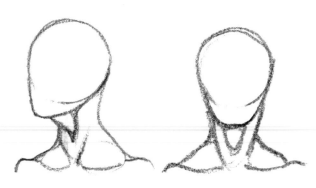

When you're connecting the head to the body remember that the neck is much bigger than is often anticipated—it's a huge, complex pillar of muscle, bone, and piping that supports the whole head, not a thin tube that sits on the shoulders. The bones and muscles of the neck and shoulders are very close to the surface of the skin; the muscles wrapping around from jaw to collar bone and the line of the collar bone itself can be very useful for proportioning the head with the shoulders. The head often sits surprisingly close to the shoulders, which have a coat hanger-like shape to them from the front.

Other features further characterize the head. The ear acts as a pivoting point on which the head tilts, the bottom line and front edge of the nose will give the face direction; the eyebrow line will give it tilt. The eye and mouth will give it identity and expression.

When your drawing time is limited, think about what your drawing is for, what information the drawing needs to convey, and work out which characteristics you need to include.

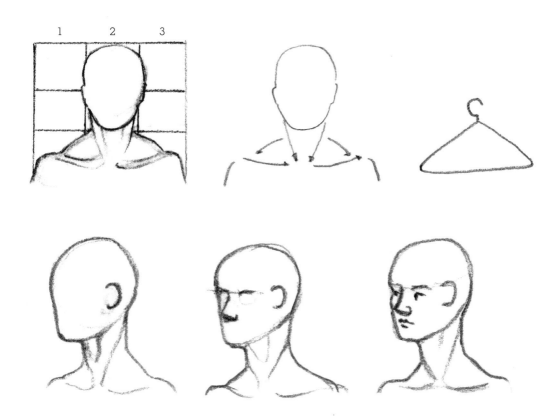

The Face

Don't be intimidated by the face. Just like any other part of the visual world, it can be simplified into shapes and lines. As human beings we have developed an astounding sensitivity to the nuanced expressions, proportions, and individual differences of the human face. When we look at a picture of a face, we bring that critical awareness to bear on it and recognize any tiny inaccuracies in the drawing. It helps to have an order to work through when drawing the face.

Frameworks and Features

At the construction stage it can help to lay down a basic scaffold that you can hang the features from. Here are some basic proportions in the face—remember that every angle you draw is unique and you shouldn't use these proportions in place of proper observations. Trust the truth of your eyes.

An Order to Work Through

Once you have some loose boundaries mapped out for your face, try drawing the features in a spiral, from the eyebrow line down and around to the side. Look for the dark shapes that suggest the features.

Things to Consider

The eye line sits halfway through the face; there is often more space above the eyes than one expects.

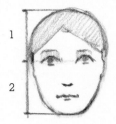

Head on, there is about an eye's width between the eyes. As the head turns, the line of the nose joins the eyebrow shape and obscures one eye, which becomes closer to the side of the face as the cheek becomes a slither.

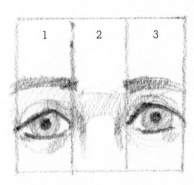

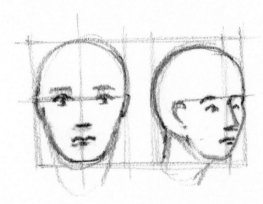

The top of the ear lines up with the eye/eyebrow, and the bottom with the base of the nose. As the head tilts backward or forward, the ear holds its position while the features move up or down. In profile, the ear is in the middle of the head, at the end of the jaw line.

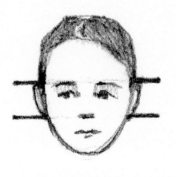

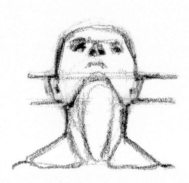

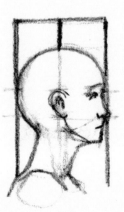

Drawing the Features

When you draw the features of the face, think about the proportions between them—the triangle between the edge of the eyes and bottom of the nose, or the vertical relationships between features.

Eyes

Nose

Mouth

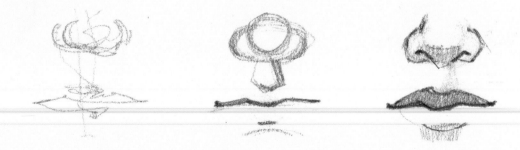

All Together

Hair and Hats

Don't underestimate how much space hair takes up on the head. In profile, the hair may cover half the surface you can see. Long hair and big hairstyles will reshape the perceived form of the head. Don't try to draw hair as little lines coming out of a scalp. Instead think about three important characteristics: shape, tone, and texture.

Shape

Look at the outline of the shape of the hair. If the border of the hair is uncertain, just make a decision about where you'll draw the border. Think about different flowing masses in the hair and break it down one shape at a time.

Tone

Even blonde hair is often darker than light skin. Dark skin is often accompanied by even darker hair. If the hair looks darker than the skin, draw it darker. You can use simple, tonal mark-making to start with, in one consistent direction, or drawn in the direction of the flow of the hair. Don't worry about whether it is curly, straight, etc., just think about getting the tone balanced correctly with the face.

Shape   Tone

Texture

Finally comes the hair texture. As you've already developed shape and tone in the hair, you can affect the feel of the hair with relatively few marks. Practice marks that suggest the rhythms you see in your subject's hair, and then use those marks selectively to create an impression of texture, concentrating on the boundaries between areas of light and dark. Use an eraser to bring light back in where needed.

Texture

Hats

When drawing any headgear think about the shapes that make up the hat and, how those shapes relate to the basic shapes of the head. Bear in mind that a hat encircles the whole head.

Arms

Bare arms and legs give insight into the anatomy beneath the clothes. See limbs as separate shapes in space, connecting jigsaw-like with the clothed form to make the complete impression of the body, and simultaneously be aware of them as the continuation of the figure beneath those clothes.

Our arms and hands reach out into the world—they are our way of pulling things to us and of interacting with our surroundings. They can operate independently of one another or in tandem. When drawing the arms, be aware that they can only bend at the shoulder, elbow and wrist—it is easy to get to caught up in the undulations of the arm and draw an arm with no bones. Identifying these joints as landmarks helps you to proportion the arm. At the construction stage, use tangents to join the landmarks, giving volume to the arm and creating a sharp point for the elbow. The upper part of the arm bulges with muscles, for lifting, pulling, climbing; the lower part of the arm tapers to the wrist, with bones closer to the surface and tendons to operate the hand.

Establish

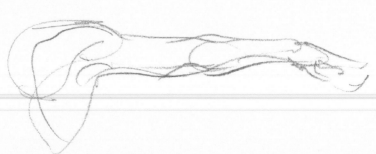

Construct: landmarks

Construct: tangents

Think about: bones

Construct: muscular flows

Think about: muscles

Elaborate

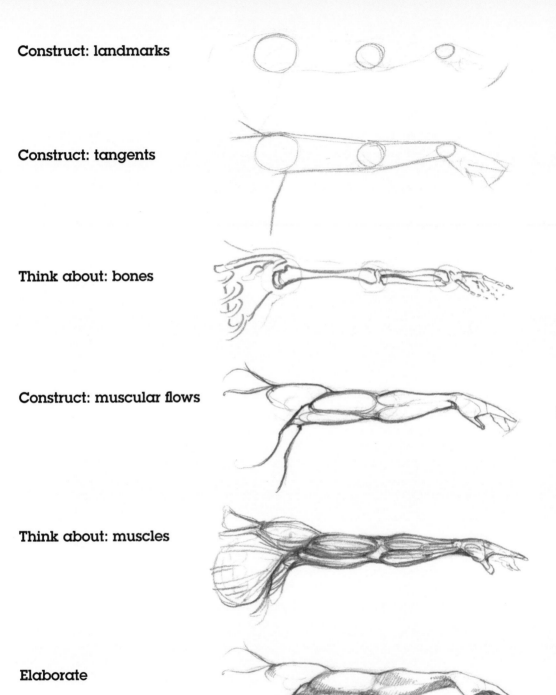

Hands

It is easy to draw hands too small—they are often larger than you think. If the hand is part of a whole figure you might only have a minute or even a few seconds to jot it down. Look at its overall shape and break down the form. If you have no time to get into detail, draw it as a simple block, paying attention to the position of the wrist, knuckle line, and the end of the fingers. When you have time to study the hand on its own, think of it like a minature figure striking little hand-poses.

Sculptor's Approach

When you start drawing the hand, you want to establish some limits for the hand's shape. Identify the position of the wrist, and jot down an underlying circular shape if it helps you. Look at the farthest tips of the fingers, the limits of the hand, and line them up with other parts of your drawing. Think like a sculptor carving the hand from wood—first you need to rough out the overall shape, then chip away at details like the fingers.

   When you're establishing the hand, think about the flow of the arm into the hand, the gesture flowing through the arm, and the intention of the pose—is it a languid arm? A dancer's gestural sweep? Is it grasping for something? At the construction stage you'll want to find several elements, such as the wrist, the block at the back or palm of the hand, the knuckle (or mitten) of the fingers, and the shape of the thumb. Divide this mitten shape into fingers and thumbs, thinking about the negative spaces between them. Refine the finger shapes as you elaborate on the forms.

Establish

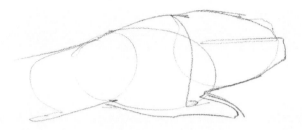

Construct: mitten

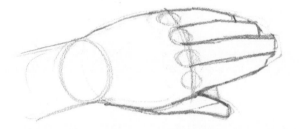

Construct: divide

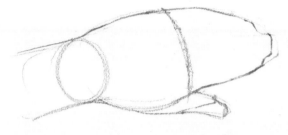

Think about: anatomy

Elaborate

Legs

The legs and feet support the figure—we're bipedal animals and our relationship with the surrounding world is rooted in the stable planting of our feet. It is easy to neglect feet in figure drawings as the head, torso, and hands hold the greatest interest and keep our attention to the top of the body. A complete figure drawing takes proper account of legs and feet.

Firstly, the legs and feet take up more space than you expect. In a standing pose, the hips and legs take up half of the whole figure and the foot is the length of the forearm (from inner elbow to wrist). We often underestimate the size of the feet because they are so far away from our faces— we're always seeing them at a distance!

Unlike the arms, which are separated by the shoulders and neck, the legs meet at the top and tend to act in tandem. The tilt of the hips and the positions of knees and ankles in relation to one another tell you a lot about how a person is supporting their weight. The upper leg is muscular and the muscular flows wrap around from the buttocks, as well as creating lines of tension down and across the leg. The bony parts of the leg are in the knee, shin and foot, with the foot being perceived as a simple block with three roughly triangular planes—the position of the heel, ankle, and the end of the toes are most important.

The knee is a big mass with a kneecap at the front. When the leg is bent, the relaxed muscle and fat of the leg distorts the leg's shape to create unusual abstract forms, often appearing very blocky and square at the knee.

Establish

Construct: landmarks

Construct: tangents

Think about: bones

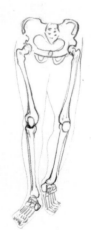

Construct: muscular flows

Think about: muscles

Feet and Shoes

The blocks of the feet have three planes to them—a triangle on the inside foot, running from ankle to heel to big toe; a sloping plane on top of the foot; and a triangular underside, the side which makes footprints in sand. The toes make another wedge that can be easily divided up. When you're trying to make sense of the foot just think about which planes you are seeing. The position of the heel in relation to the ankle is important—the line of the Achilles tendon can help you connect the two. The lower leg is critical to how we see the foot; the back of the legs bulge, with the calf muscles tapering to the ankle and tendons operating the toes from farther up the leg. The shin is seen as a hard edge of bone running down from the knee, contrasting with the muscular flows elsewhere in the leg.

Shoes

Some shoes are molded around the foot, while some shoes reshape and reposition the foot. Shoes with heels significantly change the relationship between ankle and heel, creating different rhythms in the whole leg. Think about the sculptural qualities of shoes in their own right, and try drawing them without people wearing them. Then consider what they add to a pose, for instance hiking boots provide grip and stability—in a drawing they may prove a visual anchor, creating extra weight at the end of the leg. Heels may imply a tottering pose or create elegant flow in the figure, while streamlined trainers might create a casual impression or suggest flexibility and potential imminent movement. Socks create lovely abstract shapes to draw.

Establish

Construct: landmarks

Construct: planes

Construct: divisions and flows

Elaborate

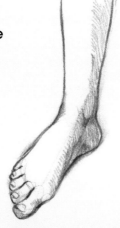

Clothing

The clothes we wear have a practical purpose and aesthetic value. They might keep us warm or protect us from the sun; they might accentuate aspects of our figure we wish to show off or conceal those that we don't. The style of clothing we wear speaks of our position in society, our class, our social allegiances; it makes an unspoken comment about our age, our occupations, and the period in which we live.

Clothing brings fabric into figure drawing. The body of your subject is interacting with their outfit, creating new and interesting shapes to draw. Here are some important considerations to bear in mind when drawing clothing:

- What kind of shape does the garment create on the person?
- How does the garment behave on the form? Does it cling, hang, or billow?
- How does the fabric crease? What kind of fold-shapes does it create?
- What kind of surface texture does the fabric have? How does it reflect light?

Shape and Behavior

Look at the shape of an outfit and the behavior of the fabric at the establishing stage of a drawing. Look for big sweeping shapes in the garment, and consider the figure underneath and how the body is filling the shape of the outfit. Find the big shapes in the figure and garment first, then look for folds that cut through the fabric.

Establish

Construct: overall shape

Construct: big folds

Construct: big folds

Fabrics and Drapery

There are almost always creases and folds to draw in the costumed figure. Learn to filter out the smaller creases and look for big folds first. When you draw a fold don't make anything up, aim to replicate a line that you really see in front of you. Practice by draping fabric over an object and drawing it; observe how the triangular folds point toward points of tension.

Object draped with fabric:

Establish and erase

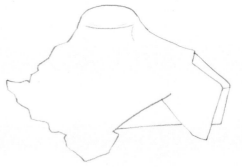

Draw outline shapes

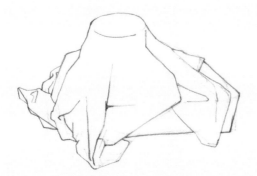

Draw lines of key folds

Draw shapes of shadows

Look at how patterns on the surface of fabric change direction as it folds. When drawing textures and patterns, don't try to interpret the pattern, just see what is there and draw it as you observe it. Regular patterns like stripes are distorted by the form beneath the clothes, contouring over curves. Draw each stripe as a shape in its own right to achieve the right illusion.

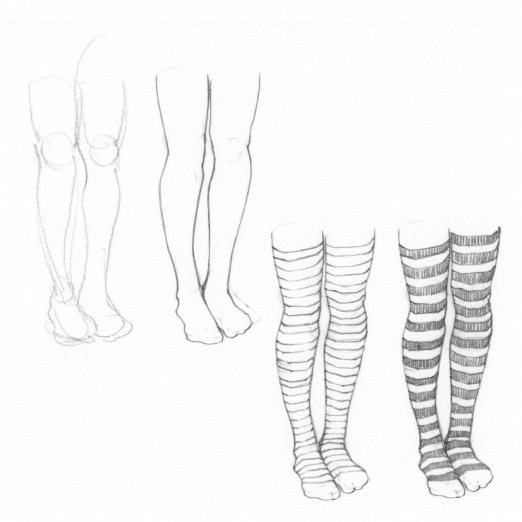

Clothing References

Dynamic Figures

If you're sketching out and about, your subjects won't always be still. Predicting and capturing moments of stillness is part of the skill of the guerilla draftsman. Think about how you can capture the movement rather than fight against it—drawing needn't always be used for recording stillness—it can be used to convey movement in figures as well.

Charting Movement

Imagine a dancer sweeping their hand through space in a smooth, continuous motion. You could attempt to draw the shape of the hand in any one of the positions you've perceived along its course, or you could draw the sweep of movement. You could even draw the two combined; drawing dancers and choreographed movement provides the opportunity.

Gesture and Flow

Gestural sketches are all about pulling the essential feel and gesture from a pose, finding the flowing lines and shapes that capture the essence of your subject. When drawing quick poses or a moving figure, set yourself a shape or line to follow and repeat, and as you watch it change try to capture the variety of its different iterations. In these drawings I've followed the costume and arm shapes in a dancing pose.

Repeated Shapes

People often repeat their movements—a sunbather on the beach might fidget, but they'll often return to the same position. When a person walks, their feet move ahead of one another in repeated movements, creating shapes in space that can be drawn a little more each time they reoccur. Look for repetitive movements so you can improve at sketching them quickly, and continue your unfinished drawings later.

Partial Figures

There's nothing wrong with a partial figure study. If your unwitting subject moves, try drawing somebody else, or find the shapes in their new position. Some drawings will be more successful than others, but many partial figures drawn on one page can be engaging in their own right.

Age

In a drawing, posture, context, and clothing can imply age as much as wrinkles or smoothness of the skin.

Babies

Drawing babies from life is fun, but challenging. Draw them asleep to capture them still, or embrace their wriggles and fidgets by making a page of gestural studies. Expect their proportions to be different, with relatively bigger heads and more convex lines in podgy limbs.

Children

Children have smoother skin than adults and it is easy to make them look too old. If you're trying to draw children from life you might have the most success sitting sketching a profile while they watch TV, or embracing the energy of their activities while making quick studies of them.

Elderly

Elderly faces and hands contain the character of a long life and a person's experiences—drawing from an elderly model can be a wonderful opportunity for conversation and reflection.

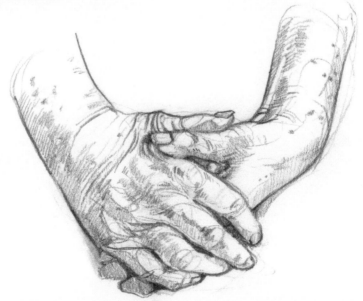

Landmarks and Mannequins

As you break down your simplistic schema of the figure through regular observational drawing you will find yourself starting to develop a new understanding of the body based on your observations. It is as if you were swapping the little two-dimensional cartoon figure in your head for a fully articulated mannequin. You can use this understanding to help you solve problems in your drawings, and it is this kind of visual knowledge that professional animators and figurative illustrators often develop to allow them to draw realistically without reference. There is a distinction to be drawn between unhelpful knowledge that stands in the way of clear seeing, and helpful knowledge that aids your observation of the figure.

Finding Landmarks

You develop the "internal mannequin" by learning to identify landmarks in the figure. These are generally joints or big bone masses, and so relate directly to knowledge of the skeleton. A more advanced understanding builds on knowledge of muscular flows in the body and surface shapes where fat builds up. By looking for and drawing these shapes you become more sensitive to seeing them—practice laying them out from memory and then moving them around to create frameworks for articulate figures.

Two-dimensional figure   Articulated mannequins

Pros and Cons

A well-developed "internal mannequin" can take years of observational drawing to formulate and not everybody will draw in a way that promotes this kind of understanding of the figure. But if you ultimately want to draw figures from your imagination, it is crucial to develop a strong internal concept of the body's articulations. However, relying on an internal mannequin when drawing from life can encourage you to be lazy with your observations or use generic devices in place of genuine observation. It is up to you to decide the best approach for the situation.

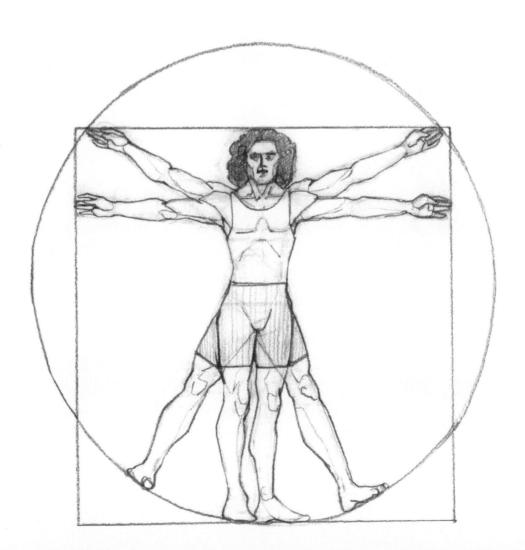

Human Proportions

The classic drawing by Leonardo da Vinci of the Vitruvian Man shows a figure encapsulated in geometric shapes. Artists have often sought to understand the ideal proportions of the human figure, and to gain insight into the essential nature of beauty. Sometimes beauty lies not in idealization, but in a truthful rendition of the observed world, albeit through the illusory lens of drawing.

Study and explore the variety of the human form—the poses people adopt will affect your perception of their bodies as much as their physical proportions.

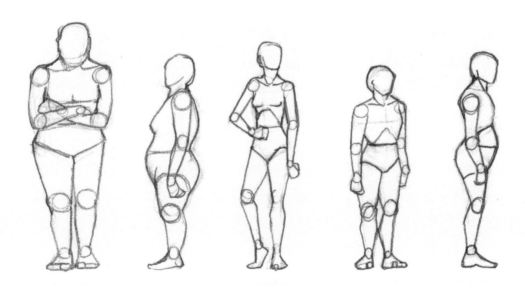

Here are some common proportions that you might expect to see in average human figures; they will differ for every person you draw, and each pose will redefine your understanding of these proportions, so trust your eyes first.

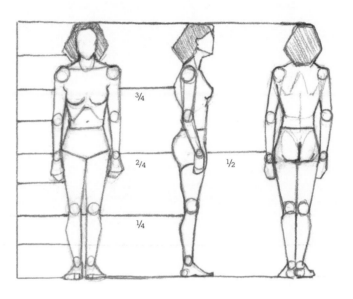

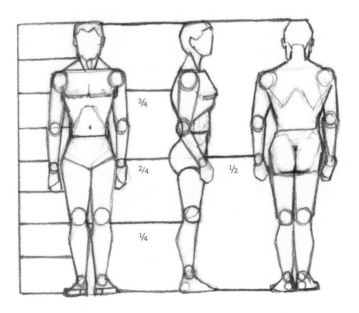

Masculine/Feminine

There are broad differences between the average male figure and average female figure that we can talk of as masculine and feminine characteristics. However, it is important not to confuse the general with the particular—female bodies have masculine characteristics, and male bodies feminine characteristics. Each individual's body is very different and much of our perception of gender comes from the clothing, pose and social context. If you're trying to accentuate masculine and feminine characteristics in figures then think about some of these broad differences.

- On average masculine foreheads slope back more than flatter feminine foreheads.
- Masculine brows tend to be heavier with less space between the eyebrow and eye.
- Feminine jawlines describe smoother curves across the face, in contrast to a squarer masculine jaw.

Typical Male Adults

Masculine toros typically tend be blockier in appearance, with broader shoulders and less variety of shapes between hips and shoulders. Think about where fat is put on around the body when drawing.

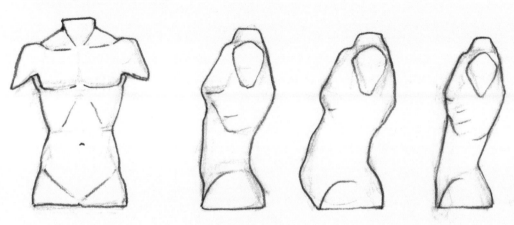

Typical Female Adults

Feminine shoulders tend to be less square than masculine shoulders, with the torso tapering more at the waist in slim figures and comparatively broader hips. Breasts create unique shapes in the chest that are not present in the same way in men, and it is worth noting the difference in body shape during pregnancy.

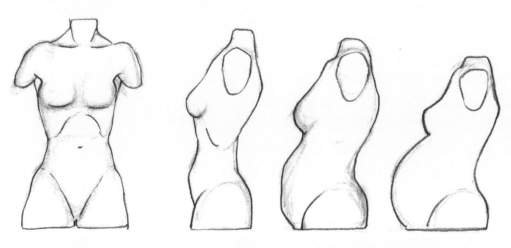

Foreshortening

Foreshortening is a word used to describe the optical distortions created by the effects of perspective on an object—chiefly that a length along the line of sight will appear relatively shorter than a comparable length across the line of sight. It is not a special kind of perspective in itself; it is a term normally used to refer to an isolated object or figure rather than an entire composition. Some degree of foreshortening is always present in observational drawing; however it is not always a significant issue. Extreme foreshortening is normally the result of being very close to the subject and can add drama or comedy to an image.

Foreshortening in a cylinder: the cylinder viewed from near the end has more compact proportions than when viewed from this side; the farthest end is drawn smaller than the nearer end.

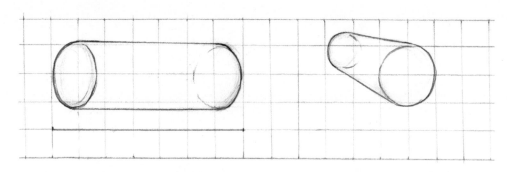

Cylinder from the side   Foreshortened cylinder

If you are observing your subject properly, foreshortening shouldn't present a problem—however, your brain often wants to interpret the subject and you may find yourself playing down the effects. If you're drawing a foreshortened figure you may find it helpful to use measuring techniques (pages 54–55) to check major distances, as well as checking the vertical and horizontal relationship between landmarks in the body.

Problem Solving

The key to improving your draftsmanship is to develop the ability to look at your drawings clearly and objectively and make judgments about changes—either changes in the drawing itself or changes in your approach to future drawings. This links in to developing an internal tutor, covered earlier in the book (page 29).

Looking at Your Drawing Afresh

While you're working on a drawing, it is easy to become too close to it—so close that you have trouble seeing it clearly. Develop your own strategies for looking at your drawing afresh. Step back from it; hold it out at arm's length to compare it to the model; treat it like a "spot the difference" and when you identify things that might be wrong, make changes to correct them. Turning a drawing upside down or looking at it in a mirror can be a good way of viewing the picture objectively and checking what might be wrong with it.

Dealing with a Problem

Once you've identified a problem, don't be afraid to revise your drawing. Always be prepared to erase big chunks of the drawing and re-draw them—if you've drawn something once it is much easier to erase it and redraw it slightly to the left or right, or up or down. Don't be too precious—if you really like one eye but it is out of proportion with the rest of the face, don't try to make the drawing work around it; erase it and make everything work together. If you don't, you'll only be unhappy with the final result anyway. Keep your bad drawings as well as your good ones. As you look back over your many drawings you may notice that you repeat the same mistakes; this is a good thing as you can identify and then work out how to deal with them.

Common Problems

Here are few common problems and some visual tips on how to deal with them.

Problem: The head doesn't fit the body.

Short-term solution: Return to the head, re-draw the silhouette, and then expand the features to fit.

Long-term solution: If you're adding the head last, try incorporating it into the rest of the pose earlier, treating it almost as another limb. If you're drawing it first, the disproportion is likely happening when you draw the shoulders; check the proportions here before moving on.

Problem: Parts of the figure are in proportion with one another but not with surrounding body parts.

Short-term solution: Pick one area as your core area; erase all body parts that aren't in proportion with that area and re-draw them using that area to proportion from.

Long-term solution: Make sure the whole figure is well plotted out at the construction stage; don't work from one area of small details to another, but keep zooming back from the pose and seeing it as a whole.

Problem: Figure appears off-balance.

Short-term solution: Find the line of weight in the figure, running from the head down through the feet. Re-draw parts of the figure to align better with that flow. Add a shadow underneath the figure to connect it to its environment.

Long-term solution: It is important to jot out the top and bottom of the pose early on and to relate the top extremity, such as the head, to the lowest extremity, such as the foot. Line up the heel and toe with landmarks vertically above them and make sure the foot is large enough.

References

Exploring Drawing

If this book has helped give you a taste for drawing, the best way to keep improving is to find a community of other people who also love to draw. There's nothing better than finding a bunch of people who share the joyful revelations of looking and sketching and who have experienced and overcome the same obstacles inherent in learning to draw.

Many adult education centers offer structured courses in portrait or life drawing and most towns will have small art societies. Drop-in life drawing classes and drawing clubs can be a sociable way to draw and meet others who draw, and an internet search will often yield a wealth of groups in your area.

The Sketchcrawl movement hold regular group sketching events around the world and the Campaign for Drawing list drawing events in the UK and internationally as part of their Big Draw initiative. I run classes at various institutions in London and through my own drawing school, Draw Brighton. If you can't find anywhere suitable, consider setting up your own group, where you can take it in turns to model for portraits or share the cost of a professional artist's model. If you'd like to share your drawings on social media you can tag them #drawpeople

Recommended drawing books

Anatomy for the Artist by Sarah Simblet
The Craft of the Lead Pencil by Mervyn Peake
The Natural Way to Draw by Kimon Nicolaides
Drawing Projects by Mick Maslen & Jack Southern
Draw Faces in 15 Minutes by Jake Spicer

Online Resources

Draw Brighton www.draw-brighton.co.uk
Jake Spicer www.jakespicerart.co.uk
Sketchcrawl www.sketchcrawl.com
The Big Draw www.thebigdraw.org

Twitter and Instagram
@BrightonDrawing
#drawpeople

Acknowledgements

I'd like to thank Hester Berry, Shelley Morrow, Laura Burgess, and Mary Martin for their enduring support at Draw Brighton. I'd also like to thank Duncan Cromarty for constant feedback, John T. Freeman for his early support and ongoing input, and Tammy Cherriman and my family for indulging my life-long love of drawing.

I'd especially like to thank my models for this book: Laura Burgess, Tim Patrick, Laura Nenonen, Nick Devenish, Charlotte Miller, Marina Ray, Marion Neville, Nick Breakspeare, Milo Hartnoll, Francesca Cluney, Emma Sandham King, Lucy Clougherty, Mary Martin, Dave and David, Emily Rose, Kane Cherriman, Greg Smith, Oscar Spicer, Lauren Heckler, Soumen Basak, Collette Tarbuck, Cleo Dibb, Claire Skye Matthews, Keith Mercer, Niharika Jha, Laura Kate O'Rourke, and Felix Clement.

Finally, thanks to Roly, Zara, Emily, and the team at Ilex Press; especially Nick, for his saintly patience.

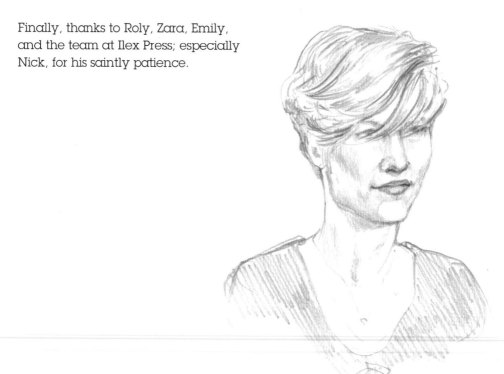